FINISHING LINE PRESS

www.finishinglinepress.com

Shape and Shadow

poems by

Linda McClure Dunn

Finishing Line Press
Georgetown, Kentucky

Shape and Shadow

ACKNOWLEDGMENTS

An earlier version of "Keeping Up Appearances" appeared in *Muscadine
Lines: A Southern Journal.*

This book would not exist without the support and inspiration of so many:
my first writing group, "Women Who Write Loudly"; Connie Jordan Green
and members of her chapbook workshop; Darnell Arnoult and members
of her novel workshop and critique group; Sue and Harry Orr who provide
space conducive to the process; and talented teachers and authors who have
generously shared their knowledge and experience. I am more than grateful
for the patience and belief of Martin and the family as I pursued this venture
to a conclusion that often seemed unlikely.

Publisher: Leah Maines
Editor: Christen Kincaid
Cover Art: Linda McClure Dunn, Sculptor; C. Martin Dunn, Photographer
Author Photo: C. Martin Dunn
Cover Design: Elizabeth Maines McCleavy

Printed in the USA on acid-free paper.
Order online: www.finishinglinepress.com
also available on amazon.com

Author inquiries and mail orders:
Finishing Line Press
P. O. Box 1626
Georgetown, Kentucky 40324
U. S. A.

Table of Contents

We are what we are given
and what is taken away ...

Wendell Berry, from "The Gift of Gravity"

Inclusions

They float within me
like lava lamp globules
in tremulous suspension,
erupt suddenly on the surface—
imprints from past generations,
traits as innate as my blue eyes.

Widow: 1943

I wonder how Granny did it alone
on the farm. Rising daily at dawn,
chores called her no matter the weather.
Arthritis and age nagged body and soul.

On the farm she rose daily at dawn,
making do with what was at hand.
Arthritis and age nagged body and soul,
her loneliness deeper than crowds could fill.

She made do with what was at hand,
pieced memories together like scraps in her quilts.
With a loneliness deeper than crowds could fill,
companionship lay in her Bible and books.

She pieced memories together like scraps in her quilts.
Chores called her no matter the weather.
Companionship lay in her Bible and books.
I wonder how Granny did it alone.

Yankee Patrol
A Family Parable of Duty

Horses coming around the bend,
riders more likely in blue than gray,
sparse Georgia pines on either side—
no place to hide for a Rebel boy
bearing supplies to his soldier brothers.
No place to hide but under the bridge,
rickety bridge over dried up creek,
crouch low in a hollow at its base.

Rhythmic cadence across the planks,
legs and boots flash in spaces between.
His heart pounds fierce as the hooves above.
Will they take a child, force him to tell
where he is going and what he carries?
Discovery certain, he vows to God
he will die brave before he will tell.

Then silence so sudden his heart drowns it out.
The enemy gone, he wishes for home
and his mother's embrace, wipes his nose,
leaves his shelter, his errand still waits.

Capitulation

Sudden rainstorm, open windows
I hurry to close, see the bird pelted
by raindrops the size of his head.
Tail a rudder swinging in waves of wind,
his tiny toes lock on the gyrating red feeder.
Hummingbird takes what he needs to survive.

Why can't I cling to what nourishes me?
Time—to release words from my mind,
words prone to fade in a Hoover's hum.
No one goes naked minus one load of laundry,
nor starves if the grocery trip waits.
Lunch could be late, dust rest 'til tomorrow.

Do I claim obligations, or they claim me?
Pushing ahead of creative impulse,
they sting my conscience
like raindrops pelting my face.
I close the window. A metaphor, too?
Perhaps a poem for another day—

Inheritance

Grandfather died at an early age,
my father too young to know him.
Pictures found in a dusty box
hold clues to the man he was.

A portrait in fading gray tones poses him,
pale shirt blends into darker vest, tie a graceful bow.
Thin, mustachioed gentleman sits tall,
long fingers curve over velvet chair arm;
Bible on table beside him.

An outdoor family scene, sharp contrasts
of light and shadow reveal disheveled farmer.
Beneath the mustache lurks a sneer, drunken
defiance of gravity in the wooden chair
he cocks back on two legs.

Grandma sits erect nearby
unsmiling, oblivious to his presence
or the crying baby on her lap;
five stair-stepped little soldiers
stand attention by her side.

Strengths, faults, infused behaviors
so obvious in black and white,
flow down the generations—revealed
by involuntary actions, expressions. All of us,
like Grandfather, best observed in shades of gray.

Early Disillusion

Through all its seasons
I watched the pussy willow,
but no kittens grew.

Storybooks promise
delightful places and things
but never tell true.

Traces

Dew drops on grass are tiny flash bulbs
blinking in breezy morning light,
pecan tree a dancing green mosaic;
my spirit refuses to stir.
I sit on calming cool of concrete steps,
sip coffee, steel myself for another vigil
beside Gran slipping slow into release.
My drifting eyes are drawn to shadow patterns
through the grass tracing the outline
of a house razed years ago—

a concave path where herringboned bricks led
through Gran's velvet-dark roses gives way
to furrows along porch-edge, around the corner
to bedroom walls whose floor-length windows
welcomed winter's warm afternoon light,
framed summer's zinnias against whitewashed fences.
Laughter and mantle clock chimes echo again
against high ceilings while I learn Bible stories,
Greek legends, canasta, quilt-piecing;
how the life force frees chicks from eggs
in a shoe box behind the stove.

I see the depression bereft of tree roots
where a black walnut presided
over backyard mysteries of laid eggs,
buried bits of old potato making new ones,
and flowers becoming pears.
It shaded worn wooden steps where family tales
were accompanied by the rhythm of shelling peas.

Those who built walls and walks,
planted zinnias and roses, told stories,
lost their tangible forms as did things they made.
But I, like this piece of earth I'm settled on,
bear indelible marks of strong foundations laid.

Transient Child

Where am I from?
Who are my people?
The answer won't mean much to you.
Dad's work takes us far
from where family began.
Here for the moment, two parents and me
comprise a makeshift security.
Friends aren't forever; never time to belong.
Roots found in books, on bright movie screens—
unstable to grow on, but transplant with more ease.

Game Over

Choices are chances.
Some things I chose before I knew
chance has two faces.

Photo: Freshman Co-eds 1957

Captured waiting in the Admissions line,
chatting about our dread of Saturday classes;
no two of us are the same, yet all alike
in cuffed socks, dirty bucks, or penny loafers.
Snug sweater sets and straight wool skirts reveal
as much as prudence allows, clothes too warm
for Deep South autumn but it's the college look.
We wear new watches and grandmas' rings
given for graduations or eighteenth birthdays,
and invisible, but surely clasped upon us,
chastity belts forged from society's steely conventions.

In gender-specific dorms musty still from summer,
plush tigers sporting colors of purple and gold
share twin beds with strewn contents of suitcases
brought to support expectations more dear
to Depression-era parents than ourselves.

Most courses keep us snuggled in the past
while Sputnik drifts overhead on nights
when Castro's guerrillas slip in and out of the hills
and frat house bands fracture Larry Williams' lyrics—
got the walkin' pneumonia and the Asiatic flu.
Greek rush is prioity; gas is 24 cents so we go
anywhere, anytime, in conspicuously-finned convertibles,
but aware the housemother's suspicious eye waits
to inspect us as we sign in at curfew.

We sense the cultural shift. Boys liberate Playboy
from under beds where mother will not be sweeping.
They take liberties they assume we expect;
we are aroused by adventure more than lust,
indignant faced with choices we thought predetermined.
The Army drafts Elvis; adulthood threatens.
Space wars morph from fantasy to chilling plausibility.

Born too soon for Baby Boomers,
too late for the Great Generation,
we drift for a decade in societal no-man's land:
eschewing halcyon myths of the '50's,
fearing psychedelic freedoms of the 60's,
and settle uneasily between extremes.
Memory will take us back to wonder at our choices
though too many years will pass to allow regret.

Undercurrents

(after Larry Levis' "The Poet At Seventeen")

My youth? spent in hesitation,
fear of failure, sense of frustration.
Riptides pressed below layered calm,
balance bought in swirls of stress.
No clue escapes revealing who
rides whirlpools beneath smooth blue.

a poem is . . .

words I cannot say
dreams destroyed
hopes retained
love confessed
emotion chained
fiery rage deep within
truth I fear to know
tears behind the smile I wear
a poem is the face I would not show

Keeping up Appearances

Old vines discarded beside a road—
morning glory blossoms persist
in the habit to which they were bred,
opening to light, closing against dark,
determined, though rootless,
to preserve the illusion of life.

Morning Train Mourning

Mourning comes easily at 3:30 a.m.
Train's distant call, ripe with regret,
disturbs uneasy dreams, swells into the dark,
magnifies echo of words gone astray,
peels shadowing Time from past transgressions,
however innocently committed.
Does the train lament passengers replaced by cargo,
as I rue worn-out beliefs cast aside
on my journey through axiologies?
Does it wail for the boy with headphones
walking the track, as heedless of disaster
as you when struck by my rejection?
Remorse is companion of private night musing
before dawn's rescue brings bustling present.
What *was* recedes, what *is* will diminish; yet
train and memory have their Doppler Effect,
and mourning comes easily at 3:30 a.m.

Repairs Needed

Another deluge envelopes us
and the gutters still aren't fixed.
The translucent veil descends
but can't disguise the problem.
No channel exists to control the flow.
A rivulet circles our foundations,
deepens its path with each passing storm.
Our choice, avoidance not resolution,
so the gutters don't get fixed.
Perhaps this structure will wash away.

Urge

Moon calls tides.
My zodiac sign, water.
Moon calls me.
Unlike the Sea,
I cannot flow outward
physically.
Moon stirs
primal essence,
concealed, not denied.
It insists that I howl—
sometimes in silence,
but sometimes out loud.

Poet and Shrub: A Need for Pruning

You might say a Spring freeze got us,
this old hydrangea and me—
a season ago for it, years ago for me.

Creative sources drained,
we stand side by side,
shriveled around our edges.

Twitching roots retain
promise of another bloom.
I hold shears; summon the will
to make a cut.

Incongruity: No One's Fault, But Here We Are

This path you chose has worn me down.
I cannot travel it anymore.
    I will not.

Faithfully I followed all this way,
no looking back, no shedding tears
    for things we left.

I know this cannot be my path.
I have tried to make it so.
    I have failed.

Don't feel that you must stop with me.
A shared illusion has no strength
    to bind us.

Ahead lies something you must find
and, while I wish your longing sated,
    I lack that need.

See the cloud of starlings split and circle
to opposite horizons, land together
    for the night?

Just so, I will look for you again
when we both reach smoother ground
    at the end.

Rationale for Emotional Flexibility

There cannot be love
without regret for what must change
and love itself is not immutable.

Retrospective Above the Lake

Never joined at the hip,
always kindred souls,
we committed too young
to know what marriage meant.
We created our own definition
while the unforeseen swept across our life
like ripples disturb this lake below us.

Quiet as strangers, we sit in separate chairs,
communal space shared between us,
watching one eagle call to the other—
a fish caught, a danger spotted—
as each flies its own path
above green pines and calm water
touched, like us, by a setting sun.

So often we sit like this,
together, yet separately absorbed
by thoughts of broader paths which might
have opened to each of us alone.
Yet we, like the eagle pair, always
return to the oft-rearranged
but satisfactory nest we built together.

In the Cemetery

I. Age 5

There's a picture of me and Grandpa the only time he saw me.
He's sick; Mama bends over Gran's curlicue brass bed,
holding me out so he can touch his first grandchild.
His reaching hand is long and skinny.
I am a baby laughing.

I visit his grave with Gran and Mama.
We take a blue-painted lard can full of Gran's zinnias
to put on the red granite marker.
Gran shows me the letters spelling out names,
tells me someday she'll lie there, too.
I ask if we'll stay here long.

There's the smell of dry grass;
I hear a cow asking to be milked
and chickens clucking across the road.
The cemetery is like Gran's pasture
except it makes me feel lonely.
Grandpa's marker is smooth and pretty,
but so cold on a hot summer day.
I hope we won't stay here long.

I'm told it's disrespectful to stand on the spot
where the body is buried. I remember that picture:
me, above his reaching witch-hand,
and I retreat to the plot's concrete edging—
safe base like a game of tag.
I hope we won't stay here long.

All the way home the image lingers:
the dead man who reached from the curlicue bed
where Gran and I read stories, imagine far-away places,
say our prayers, fall asleep. How safe is that base?
I think I can't stay there long.

II. Age 55

Little changes in this place or the town it serves.
Sparse-growing grass rustles in summer wind,
cows amble in adjoining pastures,
red granite marker still smooth and cold to touch,
though Grandpa has company. Gran lies by him
as she intended; Mama and Daddy beside them,
an uncle and aunt at their feet. Bed-size hollows
have sunk over the spots where they lie.
I have returned to bury each one
but I don't stay here long.

I've wandered too far off the path to this spot.
They offered me pictures and words,
perhaps of their dreams, meant for my erudition,
not to pull me away from tradition and roots
holding them then as the ground holds them now.
Still I sense hands reaching out, as I reach back,
but understanding remains beyond our grasp.
I follow the call of the world they imagined
and I won't stay here long.

A Burning Desire

No desiccated thing would I be, boxed
underground, chemicaled, cosmetic-coated,
artificial as fake flowers on a tombstone,
found in twenty generations,
forensically probed and classified.
Release me through fire to earth, air, and water.

Find me millennia from now in sandstone strata
shaped by future wind into wondrous shapes,
elemental greens, yellows, reds, seeping through rocks;
in remnants of riotous life, limestone-locked,
where oceans formed and dried again.
Find me as atoms in up-swirling spirals of air,
coalescing into clouds, watering newer versions of life.
Return me to the infinite process.

Observations on an Autumn Evening

Low-slanting sun gilds all it touches.
Even old white horse, himself burnished,
swishes a tail of floating gold strands,
grazes on tawny summer grass remnants.
Dried leaves float down, seeking their rest,
unburden branches whose shapes are revealed
in their true patterns against a pale sky.
As day's last light blends to night's shadow,
I am content.
Seasons of life blend one to the other,
reveal things more clearly in softer light.

Linda McClure Dunn was born in a bayou-side south Louisiana town where her parents, native Texans, lived at the time. In her growing up years, her father's work as a oilfield "tool pusher" moved them through the various and culturally varied sections of the state as the drilling company moved its rigs. She spent vacation times with grandparents and other relatives in the northeastern and central parts of Texas with four generations of the family, originally early settlers of what is now the Virginia—Carolina area. Such deep and wide-spread roots have had a strong influence in her perspective on life and in her writing.

Linda wrote for fun from childhood. She graduated from Terrebonne High School in Houma, LA, focused on English and Theater for two years at Louisiana State University. She married a native of Alexandria, LA, where they lived for ten years before his work took them to Natchez, MS, and Memphis, TN, eventually settling them in Middle Tennessee in the early 1970's. A stay-at-home mom as her two children grew up, Linda was an active volunteer, often writing promotional information for civic and social organizations. Later she was employed as a feature writer for a local newspaper and did administrative work in the arts and in banking. Her interest in developing the craft of writing has come to the fore in retirement. Her work explores the interweaving of past and present.

Linda and her husband have been married fifty-eight years. They live in Franklin, TN, and enjoy a wide range of interests. In addition to words in any form, Linda loves sewing, most kinds of music, live theater, sports cars, the Pacific Ocean, mountains, ancient ruins, cosmology, football, good wine, and dark chocolate.

www.ingramcontent.com/pod-product-compliance
Lightning Source LLC
LaVergne TN
LVHW021124080426
835510LV00021B/3315